Writing to Others

SECOND EDITION

CHERI COOK

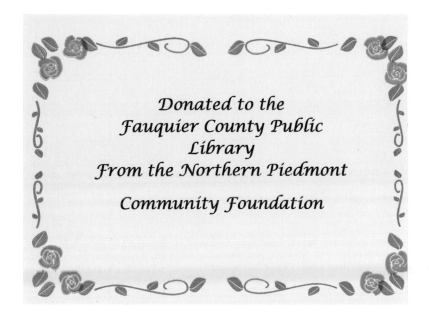

New Readers Press

Writing to Others, 2nd ed.

ISBN 978-1-56420-580-3

Copyright © 2006, 1986, 1978, 1975 New Readers Press
New Readers Press
ProLiteracy's Publishing Division
104 Marcellus Street, Syracuse, New York 13204
www.newreaderspress.com

Printed in the United States
9   8   7

Proceeds from the sale of New Readers Press materials support professional
development, training, and technical assistance programs of ProLiteracy
that benefit local literacy programs in the U.S. and around the globe.

Contributing Author: Athena Kildegaard
Content Editor: Beth Oddy
Design and Production Manager: Andrea Woodbury
Illustrations: Linda Tiff
Production Specialist: Jeffrey R. Smith
Cover Design: Carolyn Boehmer

CONTENTS

Writing Personal Notes and Letters

What: Short notes and letters, phone messages, notes to school

Audience: Friends and family or people you know

Purpose: To share information or personal news

Short Notes

Short notes are a nice way to keep in touch. Your note can share news, respond to news from a family member or friend, or just say "Hi!" Notes are simple and easy to write.

Write your note on a sheet of paper or on a card you have made or bought. Your own handwriting will make it especially personal. There is no particular form to follow.

Some occasions are perfect for a short note. You might want to say "thank you" for something someone did. You might want to congratulate someone—on celebrating a birthday or for receiving an award, for example. Sometimes you might want to express caring or sympathetic feelings.

Thank-you Notes and Notes of Congratulations

People send notes or cards to say "Thank you" for many things: birthday, wedding, and other gifts; special favors; a dinner; or a stay at someone's home. Include specific details in your notes to make them more lively and personal.

Also, include the date. The person who receives your card may want to know when you wrote it.

Here is an example of a brief thank-you note.

Short notes are a nice way to say "Congratulations!" Good times for notes of congratulations are graduation and the arrival of a new baby.

Here is an example of a note of congratulations.

June 15, 2006

Dear Mrs. Baldwin,

Thank you so much for the lovely wedding gift. The wooden salad bowl will serve us well for many years to come.

Yours truly,
Kim and Young Min Joo

May 30, 2006

Dear Maria,

Congratulations on graduating from high school! I am proud of you and your accomplishments. And I wish you the best of luck as you continue with your education.

Your loving aunt,
Elena Gonzalez

Notes of Sympathy and Caring

A member of a friend's family dies. A friend has a serious illness or accident. At such times, caring notes are welcomed.

When people are sad or troubled, they appreciate words of comfort and sympathy. We want to support them and show our concern. But sometimes it's hard to find the right words.

When someone has died

When someone has died, it may be easiest just to send the family a card with a printed message. But simply signing your name can seem cold and uncaring. Try to add your own warmhearted words.

You don't need to write a lot. In fact, it's better to write a short, sincere message than say too much. Just say how sorry you are and that your thoughts are with your friend.

Here is an example of a note of sympathy.

October 28, 2006

Dear Mrs. Rossi,

I was so sorry to hear of Mr. Rossi's death. Not only was he a fine teacher, he was always someone we students could go to when we needed help with our problems. Once when I was very discouraged, he convinced me not to drop out of school. I'll always be grateful for the encouragement and support he gave me.

Sincerely,
Marcus King

If the person who died touched your life in some special way, tell about it. You might share a specific story. Let the family know how much you appreciated their loved one. It will be a comfort to them.

If you are writing a sympathy card to someone you don't know very well, keep it short. Just expressing your sympathy will be enough.

When someone is ill or injured

Sometimes you will want to send a card to someone who is seriously ill or injured. It's best to say very little about the illness or injury. You don't know all the medical facts. Don't risk saying something that will be upsetting. Just say that you are thinking of your friend.

> Here is an example of a caring note for someone who is injured.

March 15, 2006

Dear Ed,

I was very sorry to hear of your injury and hope that you will be feeling better soon. I am thinking of you and send you my very best wishes.

Please let me know if there is anything I can do to help.

Sincerely,
Margaret

Writing a Personal Letter

Friends and relatives often live far away. You may not be able to see them or talk to them whenever you would like to. But you can "get together" by letter.

In a personal letter, you can say what *you* want. You might share news about your family. You might tell about your work or events in your life. Think about the person to whom you are writing. What would that person want to know?

Personal letters follow a certain form. Here is an example.

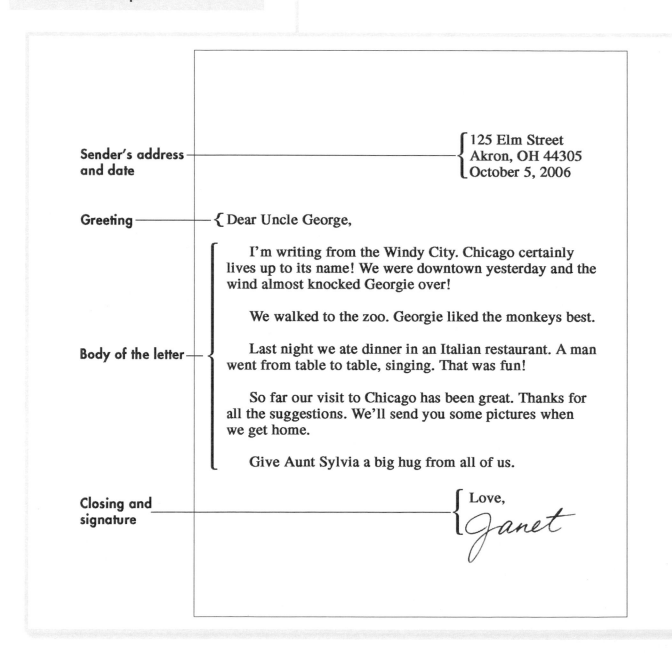

Sender's address and date

125 Elm Street
Akron, OH 44305
October 5, 2006

Greeting

Dear Uncle George,

Body of the letter

I'm writing from the Windy City. Chicago certainly lives up to its name! We were downtown yesterday and the wind almost knocked Georgie over!

We walked to the zoo. Georgie liked the monkeys best.

Last night we ate dinner in an Italian restaurant. A man went from table to table, singing. That was fun!

So far our visit to Chicago has been great. Thanks for all the suggestions. We'll send you some pictures when we get home.

Give Aunt Sylvia a big hug from all of us.

Closing and signature

Love,
Janet

Writing a Phone Message

Sometimes you'll need to leave a phone message for someone else. It is important to write accurate phone messages. Keep a pen and paper near the phone. Then you can write the message while you are still on the phone.

Always write the name of the caller. Ask if he or she would like to leave a phone number or another message. If the caller does, write down the information accurately. Repeat the number and the message back to the caller to be sure the information is correct. Write the time of the call. Sign your name to the message. Then leave it in a place where it will be seen right away.

Here is an example of a phone message.

> 1 p.m.
>
> Mike,
> John called. He can't meet you at 5:00 tomorrow. Call him. 466-6666
>
> Pete

Writing Permission Slips and Excuses

If you are a parent, you will sometimes need to write permission slips and absence excuses for your school-aged child.

Sometimes your child will bring home a form for a field trip or other school activity. All you need to do is fill in the name of your child and sign your name.

When your child has been absent from school, write an absence excuse for the child to give to the teacher when he or she returns to school. Your note needs to tell only *who, when,* and *why:*

- *who* was absent? (your child's name)
- *when?* (the day and date of the absence)
- *why?*

Put the date on the note, and sign your name.

Here is an example of an absence excuse.

> May 9, 2006
>
> My son, William Rice, missed school on Monday, May 8, because I took him to see the doctor about his injured arm.
>
> Minnie Rice

1. Thank-you note

Choose one of the situations below. Pretend you are the person described. Write a thank-you note in the box on the right.

A. You are Jim Wilson. Your friends LaShawn and Dave Jones gave you a surprise birthday party. Write a note to thank them.

B. You are Coca Hernandez. Your husband's cousin, Gloria, looked after your children for an evening so that you and your husband could go to dinner and a movie. Write her a note of thanks.

2. Note of sympathy or caring

For one of the situations below, write a note in the box on the right.

A. Your son or daughter is in Ms. Lee's class. Ms. Lee's mother has died. Write a note of sympathy to Ms. Lee.

B. You work with Elena Torres. Her husband, Jaime, is in the hospital. Write a caring note to him.

3. Personal letter

In this exercise, practice writing a short personal letter. Follow the format shown on page 8.

Write to a real friend or relative, or if you prefer, write a pretend letter.

_____

_____

_____

_____

_____

_____

_____

_____

_____

_____

_____

_____

_____

_____

_____

Writing and Responding to Invitations

What: Formal and informal invitations

Audience: Friends, family, and other people you know

Purpose: To invite people to an event or to respond to invitations from others

When you're having a small party and your guests are all close friends, you probably invite them in person, by telephone, or by e-mail. But for some parties, written invitations work better.

You might choose to send written invitations at times like these:

- when you invite more than six or eight people

- when you invite people that you don't know very well

- when the party is for someone else, such as a birthday party for your child

- when the party is in an unfamiliar location and you want to send directions

Most invitations are informal. For some events, especially weddings, invitations are usually formal.

Informal Invitations

You can write your own invitations. Or you can buy invitation cards and fill in the information. Your invitations should tell *who, what, where,* and *when:*

- who you are, if this information is needed

- what you are inviting people to (A birthday party? A baby shower? For whom?)

- where the party will be held

- when the party will be held (date and time)

Here are other things you might want to add to your invitations:

- *R.S.V.P.* If you need to know how many people are coming, write *R.S.V.P.* at the bottom of your invitations. The letters stand for French words that mean "please respond." When you write *R.S.V.P.,* people know they must tell you whether they are coming. Include your phone number or e-mail address so they can reach you.

- When will the event end? If you need the party to end at a certain time, put both a starting time and an ending time on the invitation. This is an especially good idea when the party is for young children. It lets parents know when to pick them up.

- Meal or no meal? Is the time of your party near a mealtime? If it is, make it clear whether you're serving a meal or not. For a potluck meal, be very clear what your guests should bring.

- Sometimes you may want to include something about presents. For instance, an engaged couple may have registered for gifts at one or more stores. Or a person may request that no gifts be given.

Here is an example of an informal invitation.

You're Invited!

What: A Party to Celebrate Seung-Mi's 80th Birthday!

Where: 114 Ridgeway Ave. Apartment 31

When: Friday, August 11

What time: 7:30 p.m.

Instead of a present, bring a story to tell about Seung-Mi.

R.S.V.P. jlee@abc.net

Answering Wedding Invitations

When a wedding invitation comes in the mail, should you answer it? Yes and no. For some invitations, you should tell whether or not you are coming. Here are the rules:

- You don't have to answer an invitation that is to only a wedding ceremony in a church.

- Answer the invitation if you are invited to both the ceremony and the reception.

- Answer invitations to weddings in private homes or hotels.

- Write your answer. Send it a day or two after you get the invitation.

What form should your answer take? The invitation itself will tell you. Wedding invitations can be informal, such as handwritten personal notes. Or they can be formal, such as printed invitations with many parts. Your response should be just as formal or informal as the invitation.

Answering an informal invitation

Some weddings are less formal. The couple might be married in a private home or outdoors in a park. Invitations to these weddings are often informal. An informal invitation might be written by hand. It might also be printed, but it will come without any forms or envelopes to return.

When you answer, use plain white paper and blue or black ink. Write a short, simple note. Here are examples of answers to informal wedding invitations.

> May. 5, 2006
>
> Dear Grace,
>   Carol and I will be delighted to attend Alice's wedding on the 27th.
>   We are looking forward to seeing your family again.
>
>   With love,
>   Elaine

A "yes" answer

> May. 5, 2006
>
> Dear Grace,
>   I am very sorry that we will be unable to attend Alice's wedding.
>   Our thoughts will be with you on that day. Give our best wishes to Alice and Bob.
>
>   With love,
>   Elaine

A "no" answer

Answering a formal invitation

Formal wedding invitations are printed on heavy white or cream paper. The wording usually follows a traditional form.

An invitation to the reception is usually on a smaller card. Sometimes, though, this information is at the bottom of the wedding invitation. Always respond to an invitation to a reception.

People often enclose small response cards with wedding and reception invitations. A small envelope may be included for mailing the card back to the sender. All you have to do is fill in the response card.

Here is an example of a formal, printed response card.

If there is no response card, you will need to write your own formal answer. Use your best plain white paper and blue or black ink. Look at the envelope to see who sent the invitation. Send your reply to that person.

Here are examples of formal responses.

Together with their families
Anna Maria Gonzales
and
Raul Sanchez
request the honor of your presence
at the celebration of their marriage
on
Saturday the tenth of December
two thousand and six
at two o'clock in the afternoon

Reception to follow
at Main Street Hotel
Springfield, Alabama

Mrs. Mercedes Gonzales
1213 Pleasant Valley Road
Springfield, AL 37420

The favor of a reply is requested by
November 10.
*M*_____
will____ will not____ attend
Number of persons_____

Please respond before May 15

Dawn and Simon Wilson
will_ ✓ _will not___ attend.
Number of persons attending_ 2 _.

Dawn and Simon Wilson
accept with pleasure
your kind invitation
to the wedding of Alice and Robert
on Saturday, the twenty-fifth
of May.

A "yes" answer

Dawn and Simon Wilson
regret that they are unable
to accept your kind invitation
to the wedding of Alice and Robert
on Saturday, the twenty-fifth
of May.

A "no" answer

1. *Writing an invitation*

Write an invitation to a party. Choose one of the following events. Make up the details you need.

- a birthday party for a small child
- a surprise party for a friend
- an event of your choice

2. *Answering a wedding invitation*

You have received the wedding invitation shown here. Write either a "yes" or "no" response to the invitation.

Mr. and Mrs. Gordon Morse

request the honor of your presence

at the marriage of their daughter

Jessica Rae

to

Marvin Perkins

on Saturday, the seventh of June

at three o'clock

Hotel Victoria

45 Oak Street

Albertville, California

Reception to follow

R. S. V. P.

Writing Business Letters: Form

What: A business letter that follows a standard form

Audience: Anyone with whom you do business

Purpose: To make sure the recipient takes you seriously

At times, you'll need to do personal business by mail with a company, a government agency, or an organization.

The Form of a Business Letter

A neat, clean business letter in standard form makes the recipient take you seriously. And it can help you organize your ideas.

Plan what you want to say, and write a rough draft. Make any corrections on the draft. Then make a clean copy to send.

Here are some tips for making your business letter look businesslike:

- *Paper:* Use 8½-by-11-inch white paper. Write on one side only.

- *Writing:* Type on a computer or typewriter if you can, or write in clear handwriting. Use black or blue ink.

- *Margins:* Leave at least one inch at the top, sides, and bottom of your letter. Don't crowd your writing onto one page. If you need more room, use another sheet of paper.

The sample letter below shows the parts of a business letter and where they go.
Notice the spacing between parts. Use the spacing as a guide for your own letters.

Return address
Date
{ 109 Maple Road
Cherokee, IA 51012
March 7, 2006

Inside address
{ Westvale Nursery
325 Main Street
Westvale, MT 59411

Salutation
{ To Whom It May Concern:

Please send me your spring catalog for fruit trees and berries. Also please include shipping costs for fastest possible delivery.

Thank you.

Closing
{ Sincerely,

Signature
{ *Sharon Coles*
Sharon Coles

The Parts of a Business Letter

Return address. This is your address. Include your own zip code. Use the standard postal abbreviations for state names (see page 21).

Date. This is the date you send the letter. Always include it.

Inside address. This is your recipient's address. Put it on the envelope, too.

- If you are writing to a company in general, use just the company name and address. (See the sample letter on page 18.)
- If you want a specific person to receive the letter, put his or her *full* name on the first line of the inside address. Add the job title if you know it.

> Ms. Stella Edwards, Business Manager

- If you don't know a person's name, address your letter to a job title or a department. This helps to get your letter into the right hands. For example:

> Publicity Director   Billing Department
> Northstar Computing   West Coast Delivery

Salutation. This is a direct greeting to the reader. It ends with a colon (:).

- If you know the person's name, use his or her title and last name.

> Dear Ms. Jones: Dear Senator Rush:

- Address a woman as *Ms.* unless she has another title or prefers *Mrs.*
- If you know the job title but not the person's name, use the job title.

> Dear Manager: Dear Editor:

- Use *To Whom It May Concern:* in all other cases.

Body of the letter. This is where you explain why you are writing. Come right to the point as politely and clearly as possible.

Leave an empty line between paragraphs. Paragraphs are not indented.

Closing. This ends your letter in a friendly way. Common closings include:

> Sincerely,   Yours truly,
> Cordially,   Sincerely yours,

Signature. Sign your first and last name. Type your name under your signature. If you handwrite, print your name clearly below your signature.

Addressing an Envelope

When you send a letter, you want to make sure the recipient receives it. So address the envelope carefully.

The name and address of the place or person to whom you are sending the letter goes in the middle of the lower half of the envelope. Be sure to include the zip code in the address. If you don't know the zip code, phone the post office to find out. If you know the full nine-digit zip code, be sure to use it. Also, use the correct state abbreviation (see page 21).

Your own name and address go in the upper left corner. If the letter can't be delivered for some reason, it will be returned to you.

What if you don't know the address of the company or organization? Try these resources:

- Call the reference section of your public library. The library may have business directories and telephone books from other areas.

- If you are writing about a product, call the store from which you bought it. They may be able to give you the address of the company.

- If you have access to a computer, try looking for the company or organization online.

Sharon Coles
109 Maple Rd.
Cherokee, IA 51012

Place
Stamp
Here

Westvale Nursery
325 Main Street
Westvale, MT 59411

State Abbreviations

Alabama	AL	Illinois	IL	Montana	MT	Puerto Rico	PR
Alaska	AK	Indiana	IN	Nebraska	NE	Rhode Island	RI
Arizona	AZ	Iowa	IA	Nevada	NV	South Carolina	SC
Arkansas	AR	Kansas	KS	New Hampshire	NH	South Dakota	SD
California	CA	Kentucky	KY	New Jersey	NJ	Tennessee	TN
Colorado	CO	Louisiana	LA	New Mexico	NM	Texas	TX
Connecticut	CT	Maine	ME	New York	NY	Utah	UT
Delaware	DE	Maryland	MD	North Carolina	NC	Vermont	VT
District of Columbia	DC	Massachusetts	MA	North Dakota	ND	Virginia	VA
Florida	FL	Michigan	MI	Ohio	OH	Washington	WA
Georgia	GA	Minnesota	MN	Oklahoma	OK	West Virginia	WV
Hawaii	HI	Mississippi	MS	Oregon	OR	Wisconsin	WI
Idaho	ID	Missouri	MO	Pennsylvania	PA	Wyoming	WY

1. Addressing an envelope

Use the information below to address the envelope. Remember to use state abbreviations.

The letter is from James Macalester, 3997 Wilcox Avenue, Trenton, New Jersey 08620.

The letter is to Dr. Maria Torres, Central Health Clinic, 2500 James Street, Little Rock, Arkansas 72204.

```
_____

_____

_____
```

Place
Stamp
Here

```
_____     _____

_____

_____
```

2. Writing a salutation

Write a proper salutation for each address. Use correct punctuation.

A. Manager
Starlight Ballroom
1421 Cedar Avenue
Beacon Hill, NJ 07102

_____

B. Billing Department
Upstate Power Company
677 Park Street
Chestertown, Texas 77757

_____

C. Mr. Tony Dell, Claims Department
Outlook Insurance Company
4953 Briggs Road
Hartford, CT 06117

_____

D. Dr. Martha Fisher
226 Medical Arts Building
1120 Allison Avenue
Milwaukee, WI 53227

_____

3. The parts of a business letter

Write the names of the numbered parts of the business letter on the right.

1. _____

2. _____

3. _____

4. _____

① 225 South Huron
Newton, IL 62301
April 4, 2006

② Whitney Discount Sales Company
4852 Lake Street
Minneapolis, MN 56554

To Whom It May Concern:

③ I am writing to request your most recent catalog. Would you please put me on your mailing list?

Thank you.

Sincerely,

④ *Amy Nelson*
Amy Nelson

Writing Business Letters: Content

What: An effective business letter

Audience: Anyone with whom you do business

Purpose: To make a request or express an opinion about an issue

There are many reasons for writing business letters. Here are some examples:

- to ask for information
- to make a request or place an order
- to express an opinion
- to solve or avoid a problem
- to show your interest in something

In a business letter, it is very important to write clearly and simply. In the first sentence, tell *why* you are writing. Next, explain *what* you need. Include necessary details, such as dates and I.D. or invoice numbers. Request specific action if that is appropriate. Then end the letter politely. Be as brief as you can.

Check grammar, punctuation, and spelling carefully. If possible, ask someone else to proofread your letter. Errors can cause your reader to take you less seriously.

Requesting Information

One useful type of business letter is a request for information. Write such letters when you need the following:

- information about a product you have bought or one you want to buy

- information about services such as those provided by the phone company, a school, your bank, or your power company

Keep your letter short, and state clearly what you want to know.

Here is an example of a letter asking about a product. This writer wants to replace a part. You could also ask about a product you want to buy. How much does it cost? How is it shipped? Where can it be repaired?

When you are asking about a specific product, include the make, model number, and serial number if you know them.

Here is an example of a letter asking about a service.

You might want to write to an organization for reasons like these:

- to order catalogs and brochures from schools, museums, parks, vacation destinations, etc.

- to request information about services offered by businesses such as phone companies, banks, medical practices, or law firms. For example, you might ask your bank about savings programs for children.

- to request phone numbers, e-mail addresses, maps, or business hours

6655 Wilson Drive
Dupont, NM 34487
October 7, 2006

Toast-R-Magic
1200 North Blvd.
Ripley, WV 25271

To Whom It May Concern:

I need a replacement part for my Toast-R-Magic countertop toaster oven, Model SD-5100. My oven's serial number is 577-011-664.

Is it possible to buy a replacement grill rack? The store where I bought the oven does not carry replacement parts.

Please tell me the cost and where I should send my order.

Thank you.

Sincerely,
Jo-In Lee
Jo-In Lee

230 Spruce Court
Ida, SD 21135
March 23, 2006

State Parks Commission
State Office Building
Helena, MT 59620

To Whom It May Concern:

Please send me the following information about camping facilities at Big Arm State Park.
- Are reservations necessary? If so, how far in advance do you need them?
- What are the camping fees?
- Are all campsites equipped with electricity?

Please send any brochures and maps about the park that you have available. Thank you.

Sincerely,

Joseph Bear
Joseph Bear

Placing an Order

A business letter can be used to place an order. As with all business letters, state your request immediately. Keep your letter short and write clearly.

Catalogs usually include order forms. Sometimes, though, you may want to order something when you don't have a catalog. Write a letter to place your order. Give as much information as you can.

- the name of the product
- the model number
- size, color, or style
- how many you want

If you know the price of the product and the cost of shipping, include a check with your order. If you don't know, ask the company to send you a bill or invoice.

Always keep a copy of your letter.

Here is an example of a business letter that places an order.

Some orders are not for products. For instance, you might order tickets for a concert or program. Remember to keep your letter short and to clearly explain what you want.

14 Summer Street
Syracuse, NY 13210
January 16, 2006

Midwest Blue Notes
4458 Circle Drive
Kansas City, MO 48920

To Whom It May Concern:

I would like to order two CDs by the band "Twist." I believe the CDs are titled "Twist Under the Stars" and "Sheer Twisted Blues." If you can ship them and bill me at the address above, please do so. If not, then please send me prices and shipping costs for these CDs.

Thank you,
Donna Witherspoon
Donna Witherspoon

Writing Letters of Complaint

Sometimes you need to speak your mind and complain. Like all business letters, a letter of complaint needs to get right to the point. What are you complaining about? Explain the situation. Then state the action you want taken.

In a good complaint letter, the writer "keeps cool." Show that you're upset, but don't be rude. Use facts and information to explain what is wrong.

Make sure you're writing to the right person. A reference librarian can help you identify that person, who might be a manager, a human resources director, or a public relations officer.

Here is an example of a well-written complaint letter.

You might want to write a letter of complaint at times like these:

- when a service has been stopped or changed without your permission—for example, if the city no longer sprays for mosquitoes in your neighborhood, or if your bank begins charging a fee for debit card use

- when a problem needs to be addressed, such as potholes in the road or a stop sign missing from a neighborhood street

- when you see something being done that is unfair or unjust, such as police giving speeding tickets only to people under age 20

3311 Western Boulevard, Apt. 6
Wilmington, IL 69891
November 8, 2006

Billing Department Manager
Wilmington Power and Light Company
1434 Sunset Avenue
Wilmington, IL 69891

Dear Manager:

Four months ago, I moved out of apartment #2, 1321 Weaver Place, Wilmington, IL. But I continue to receive electric bills for that apartment.

I notified Wilmington Power and Light to turn off the electricity on June 30, 2006. The new tenant, Anthony Wales, requested that the electricity be turned on as of July 1.

Since then, I have received four electric bills for the apartment. Now I am told my electricity will be shut off in 30 days if I don't pay both my current bill and the past-due bills for the Weaver Place apartment. I do not intend to pay an electric bill for an apartment I don't live in.

I have called your office once a month since I received the July bill. No one has yet solved this problem.

Please confirm in writing that past-due and future bills for apartment #2, 1321 Weaver Place, are not my responsibility.

Yours truly,

Mehdi al-Saaf
Mehdi al-Saaf

Writing Letters to Government Officials

Writing to elected officials is one way of getting them to represent *you*. After all, that is their job. They have to listen to the voters who elected them.

You can write to an elected official at any level of government. You can write to your city mayor or city manager. You can write to the president of the United States.

Write to the elected official who would be most likely to act on your ideas. It could be the person who serves your area. It could be a person who is working on laws that you are interested in. Or it could be someone who has said or done something you want to praise or complain about.

In letters to government officials, write about one issue. If you have something to say about another issue, write another letter. Keep your letter short and to the point.

The more important and powerful the elected official, the less likely he or she is to read your letter personally. But an aide to the official will read it and keep track of what voters like you have to say. You probably won't get a response.

Here is an example of a letter to a government official.

You might write to a government official for many other reasons, for example:

- to express your opinion on a public issue

- to discuss laws you think should be made, changed, or enforced

- to ask for help from a government agency

2527 Park Street
Sunnyvale, FL 26774
November 25, 2006

Ms. Lourdes Torres
City Councilor, Fifth District
City Hall
110 Main Street
Sunnyvale, FL 26774

Dear Ms. Torres:

A speed bump on the 2600 block of Elm Street would make our neighborhood safer for children. Many young families live in this neighborhood. Traffic between businesses along the 1800 and 3100 blocks of Elm has increased — there are more cars, and they are traveling faster. Elm Street has become unsafe for our children.

A speed bump would slow the traffic down. I have spoken to many of my neighbors, and they agree that a speed bump is necessary. We invite you to visit us and see for yourself how dangerous the traffic is.

Thank you for your attention to this matter.

Sincerely,

Anna Rosa Orro

Anna Rosa Orro

Writing Requests for Official Records

There are times when you will need copies of official records such as certificates of birth, death, marriage, or divorce; medical records; or records from schools. For example, when you enter a child in a new school, you may need a record of required immunizations, a copy of the child's birth certificate, and records from any previous schools.

In a request for an official record, include the event's date and the state, county, and city where the recorded event happened.

Address your letter to the right office. Usually the state health department keeps birth and death records. Marriage and divorce records are usually held by the county clerk's office. Ask your doctor's office or the county health office for medical records. And check with schools for educational records.

There may be a small charge for copies of records. Some offices require payment before they will fill a request. When your request arrives, they will bill you. When you send the fee, the office will send you the requested record.

You can learn about requesting legal records on the Internet. Use a search engine such as Google. Search for *get legal records* and include your state's name. You may be able to download a form for making your request. If not, you can write a business letter.

Here is a sample letter. A mother is writing for a copy of her son's birth certificate. Notice the information that she includes.

4466 Elmwood Drive
Pine Springs, AL 35123
April 3, 2006

Oregon Department of Human Services
800 NE Oregon Street
Portland, OR 97232

To Whom It May Concern:

Please send me a copy of my son's birth certificate.
  Name: Ha Ling
  Birthdate: March 26, 2001
  Place of birth: Forest Grove, Washington County, OR
  Father's name: Sook Ling
  Mother's maiden name: Li-lin Bao

Enclosed is a check for $15 to cover the cost of the birth certificate.

Thank you.

Sincerely,

Li-lin Ling
Li-lin Ling

1. Request information

Write a business letter about one of these subjects. Use correct form.

A. You own a Champion bicycle, model X110. The chain has broken. Write to the Champion Company requesting information about replacing the chain. The address is 620 Opportunity Drive, Dubuque, IA 52007.

B. Your child is old enough to go to preschool. Write to the Morning Sky Preschool to request information about their program, its costs, and hours they are open. The address is 9133 Old Highway 9, Vargas, NM 23387.

2. Write to an elected official

Write a letter to one of your elected officials. Write about one issue of concern to you. Here are some suggestions:

- Ask the official to support or not support a law that is being considered.
- Write about an issue such as taxes, police service, or public transportation.
- Write to ask for the official's attention to a local problem.

After you complete the next two pages of this book, you'll know what to put in the inside address.

3. Directory of elected officials

Before you can write to your elected officials, you must know who and where they are. A librarian can help you do the research. Or search the Internet for *government* with the names of your community and state, for example, *government Syracuse NY*.

A. The mayor, manager, or commissioner of your city or town

Name: _____

Title: _____

Address: _____

_____

B. Your representative in your city's lawmaking body

Name: _____

Title: _____

Address: _____

_____

C. The head of your county government

Name: _____

Title: _____

Address: _____

_____

D. Your representative in your county's lawmaking body

Name: _____

Title: _____

Address: _____

_____

E. Your governor

Name: _____

Title: _____

Address: _____

_____

F. Your representatives in the state legislature (People in all states except Nebraska have two representatives, one in each of the two houses in the state legislature.)

Name: _____

Title: _____

Address: _____

_____

Name: _____

Title: _____

Address: _____

_____

G. Your representative in the U.S. House of Representatives

Name: _____

Title: _____

Address: _____

_____

H. Your Unites States senators (Every state has two senators.)

Name: _____

Title: _____

Address: _____

_____

Name: _____

Title: _____

Address: _____

_____

Using the Internet for Business

What: Web sites and e-mail

Audience: Organizations and businesses

Purpose: To find information about an organization or a business, to place an online order, or to send a letter to the editor of a newspaper

In situations where you would have written a business letter in the past, you can do business over the Internet today.

Many government offices, businesses, and schools have their own web sites. You can often go to an organization's web site to order products, request information, and offer suggestions or make complaints.

Requesting Information

If you don't know an organization's web address, a search for the organization's name in a web resource like Google will probably lead you to their web site.

Every organization's web site is different. You will have to study each site to see whether it includes a way to make a request. If you find a link labeled *Contact Us,* go there. You may find one or more names with contact information. Or an e-mail form may pop up automatically for you to fill in. A link labeled *About Us* or something similar may include an e-mail address that you can use to reach the organization.

Here is an example web site. Find the link labeled *Contact Us.* If you actually clicked on that link, a form would appear for you to fill in and send. This is the most common way to request information over the Internet.

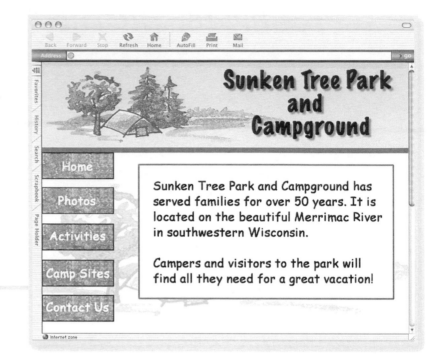

You fill in your e-mail address. You need to do only three more things:

- Add a brief subject line. Tell what the message is about. Be specific.

- Write the message. Be brief, clear, and get right to the point as you would in a business letter.

- Send or submit the message.

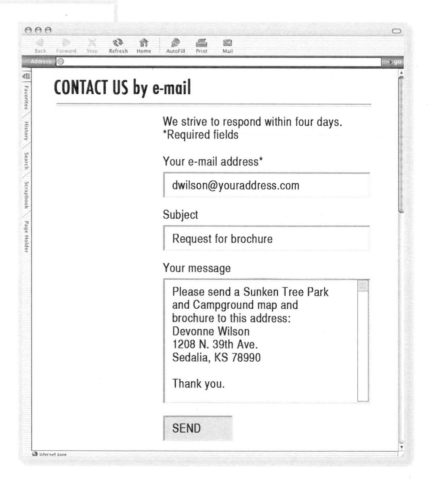

Making an Order

You can order products and services from web sites. You can order airline tickets or reserve hotel rooms for a trip. Or you can reserve tickets for events and concerts.

Be careful when you order from a web site. Consider the following guidelines:

- Order only from established businesses that have good reputations.

- Order only from web sites that use secure servers. Look at the page's URL (web address). On a secure page, the URL will start *https://* instead of *http://.* Never enter credit card information on an insecure page.

- Web sites tell you which information they require from you. Enter only that required information.

- Some web sites ask you to register and choose a password. For your protection, do not have your computer automatically remember your password.

Ordering from a web site is usually easy. Here are examples of major steps.

1. **First, choose a product. When you click *Add to Cart,* you have begun the ordering process.**

2. **When you are ready to check out, enter billing information. Notice that only starred information is required.**

3. **Finally, place your order. Before you submit it, reread the order page carefully to make sure all the information is correct. Print a copy of your order page for reference.**

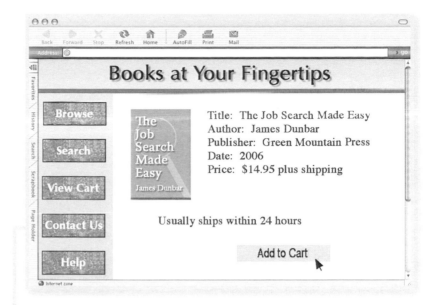

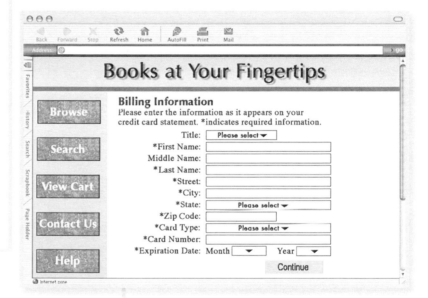

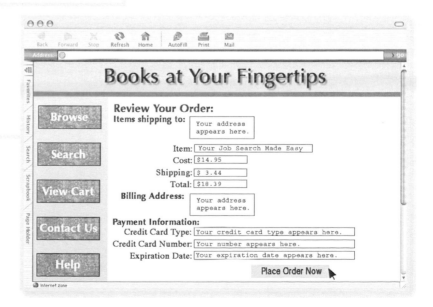

Sending a Letter to the Editor

Most newspapers today have web sites. You can read the news there. You can read other sections of the paper. You can sometimes send a letter to the editor from the site too.

Letters to the editor are a good way to share your concerns with the community. They are often written in response to something that appeared in the paper. They can also be about other current issues.

A letter to the editor should be short and clear and should come right to the point. If it refers to something that has already appeared in the paper, say that.

Here is one newspaper's computer form for submitting letters to the editor. Other papers may have similar forms.

Fill out each section of the form. Type your letter into the *Text* section. You do not need to add a salutation or a closing. When you click *Submit letter*, your letter automatically goes to the newspaper's editor.

Sometimes editors want to contact writers about their letters. That is why you are asked to give phone numbers.

It is a good idea to handwrite your letter before typing it into the form. Then you have a chance to make changes. Be sure you have said what you want to say in the clearest possible way.

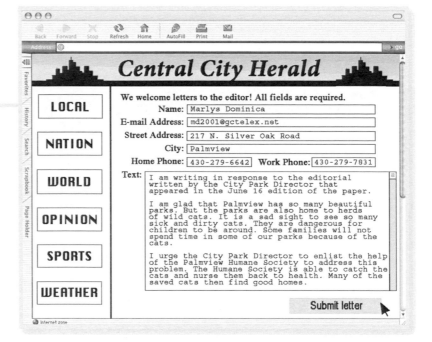

1. Requesting information

Fill out this web form to request information about car insurance offered by the First Drive Company. For this exercise, you will handwrite your request, but if you were working on a computer, you would type the request into the form.

2. Making an order

On a toy company's web site, you are ordering a clown costume for your child. You have placed the costume in the shopping cart. Now, enter the billing and shipping information. Fill the required fields in the form. For this exercise, you will handwrite the information, but if you were working on a computer, you would type it. Don't use your own credit card number here. Make one up.

Finding a Job: The Résumé

What: A summary of your experience

Audience: Anyone who hires employees

Purpose: To tell employers about you

Writing a résumé is a good first step in a job search. A résumé is a brief, organized way to show what you can do for an employer.

Before you start, think about the kind of job you would like to have. Your résumé should show that you are well qualified for that job.

Employers want to know three main things about you: your level of education, your work experience, and your work skills.

You can choose how to arrange this information. Which area best shows that you are the right person for the job you want? Put that area first on your résumé.

Under *Experience*, list your current job first. Then work back in time, listing every job you have held for the last 20 years.

Under *Education*, list your most recent education or training first. Work back to your high school diploma or GED.

Skills can be listed under specific jobs or can be listed separately. Tailor the skills you mention to the job you are seeking. Put the most important skills for the new job at the top of your skill list.

Here is a résumé for someone who has held several positions as an automotive technician. He wants to move into a job with more responsibility. He has listed his employment first because it is what most qualifies him for the job he seeks.

Dale Christian

663 W. Otter Drive   Atlanta, GA 20018   303-667-0981   dchris@abc.net

Objective: A position as lead automotive technician

Experience: AutoMax, Atlanta, GA   May 2005 - present
Assistant automotive technician
(Assistant to electrical systems specialist)
• Analyze electrical systems using computer analysis
• Replace circuit boards, processors, and chips

Superior Auto, Atlanta, GA   September 2000 - April 2005
Assistant automotive technician
(Assistant to engine repair specialist
and suspension and steering specialist)
• Tested all engine elements
• Replaced or repaired all engine elements
• Aligned front ends
• Rebuilt crankshafts

Lyle's Garage, East Point, GA   June 1997 - August 2000
Automotive maintenance technician
• Provided all general maintenance services
• Oversaw state-required automotive testing
• Sold used cars

Education: ASE certification in automotive electrical systems   2005
ASE certification in suspension and steering   2003
Automotive Certificate
  Central Georgia Vocational/Technical Institute   1998
High School Diploma
  Washington High School, Atlanta, GA   1997

References available upon request.

Here is the résumé of a person who is looking for her first full-time job. She lists her skills first because they are what most qualify her for the job she seeks. She has also included volunteer work to round out her experience.

Anna Santos

4690 North Fifth   Hayward, CT 06115   203-466-8712
santosa@defg.net

Objective: A position as telecommunicator with police, sheriff, fire, or emergency services

Skills and Abilities:
- Able to handle stressful situations
- Respectful of privacy
- Excellent communicator
- Self-disciplined
- Able to summarize information correctly
- Patient with people who are under stress or have difficulty communicating
- Fluent in English and Spanish
- Intelligent

Education:

Associate in Arts and Sciences	
Salt Hills Community College	June 2006
High School Diploma	
Emma Goldman High School, Hayward, CT	2004

Employment:

Waitress	
The Noodle Bowl	
Hayward, CT	February 2003 - August 2004

Volunteer Activities:

Tutor	
After School Stars, Salt Hills Elementary	2005 - 2006
Care Provider	
Family & Visitor Center	
Salt Hills Hospital	2004 - 2006

References available upon request.

Personal Data Sheet

On a separate sheet of paper, gather the information you need for your résumé. You may need more than one sheet of paper.

1. List your personal information.

- Your name
- Your address
- Your home phone number
- Your personal e-mail address, if you have one

It is generally not a good idea to use your work phone number or work e-mail address in a job search.

2. List your work experience. Begin with the job you currently hold or your most recent job. Then work back in time.

For each job, list the following things. It is a good idea to have all of this information at hand, even though you may not use all of it in the résumé.

- Company name, address, and phone number
- Name of your supervisor (boss)
- Job start and end dates (month and year)
- Job title
- Job duties (what you actually did as part of the job)

Under *Job duties*, mention skills or accomplishments that would qualify you for the job you are seeking.

3. List your education, most recent school first. For each item, include the following:

- Name and address of the school
- Dates you attended or date you graduated
- Subjects you studied (if they are related to the job you want)
- Name of someone at the school who could tell about your abilities

4. Make a separate list of your job skills. Include specific information about machines or equipment you know how to use. If you speak more than one language, include that. If you know how to use various computer programs, list them.

5. List any volunteer work you have done. In a résumé, include volunteer work if it applies to the job you are seeking. Also, list any honors and awards you have received.

Now you are ready to write a first draft of your résumé. Insert information from your personal data sheet into sections of the form below. Remember to begin with your most recent job and your most recent education and then work back in time. List as your objective the job you would like to have. Look at the résumés on pages 39 and 40 to see examples of proper résumé form.

_____

_____

_____

_____

_____

Objective: _____

Experience: _____

_____

_____

_____

_____

Education: _____

_____

_____

Skills: _____   _____

_____   _____

_____   _____

Volunteer Work and Honors/Awards: _____

_____

_____

References available upon request.

More on Résumés

Be accurate and neat

Before you print your résumé, read it through again. Correct any errors in spelling, punctuation, or grammar. An employer who finds even one error in your résumé may stop considering you for the job.

If you are using a computer, choose a typeface (font) for your résumé that is clean and not too fancy. Times New Roman and Palatino are good choices. Don't use fancy formatting such as shadow boxes or drawings. Keep it simple!

Look good

Choose high-quality paper, and be sure you have plenty of ink or toner in your printer. If you are typing your résumé on a typewriter, use a fresh ink ribbon.

Keep copies of your résumé in a safe place. When you need a copy, you want it to be in perfect condition.

Account for time

Time gaps in résumés worry employers. If there is a period when you were not in school and did not have a job, think about how you will account for that time. For example, maybe you quit a job to help your grandmother move into an apartment. For several months you weren't working. What should you say on your résumé?

Be sure to list any volunteer work you did during that period. Consider providing job dates by year, rather than by year and month. You might list your work experience later in the résumé to downplay the missing time. Or you could add a line or two at the end to explain the gap.

Dale Christian

663 W. Otter Drive   Atlanta, GA 20018   303-667-0981   dchris@abc.net

Objective: A position as lead automotive technician

Experience: AutoMax, Atlanta, GA   May 2005 - present
Assistant automotive technician
(Assistant to electrical systems specialist)
• Analyze electrical systems using computer analysis
• Replace circuit boards, processors, and chips

Superior Auto, Atlanta, GA   September 2000 - April 2005
Assistant automotive technician
(Assistant to engine repair specialist
and suspension and steering specialist)
• Tested all engine elements
• Replaced or repaired all engine elements
• Aligned front ends
• Rebuilt crankshafts

Lyle's Garage, East Point, GA   June 1997 - August 2000
Automotive maintenance technician
• Provided all general maintenance services
• Oversaw state-required automotive testing
• Sold used cars

Education: ASE certification in automotive electrical systems   2005
ASE certification in suspension and steering   2003
Automotive Certificate
   Central Georgia Vocational/Technical Institute   1998
High School Diploma
   Washington High School, Atlanta, GA   1997

References available upon request.

Use a computer to adapt your résumé

Typing a résumé on a computer has some important advantages. Suppose you would be happy with one of two or three different jobs. You designed and wrote your résumé for only one of them. If your résumé is stored in a computer, you can adapt it easily to fit a different job opportunity.

Here is the *Skills* section of the résumé found on page 40. Anna has never held a full-time job before. She wrote her résumé for a job as a telecommunicator.

Objective: A position as telecommunicator with police, sheriff, fire, or emergency services

Skills and Abilities:
- Able to handle stressful situations
- Respectful of privacy
- Excellent communicator
- Self-disciplined
- Able to summarize information correctly
- Patient with people who are under stress or have difficulty communicating
- Fluent in English and Spanish
- Intelligent

Anna would also be happy with a job as a receptionist. So she changed the *Skills* section to fit that position. Anna did not have to add anything to the *Skills* section, although she did shorten one item. She rearranged the list to highlight skills a receptionist would need.

Objective: Receptionist position with a small- to medium-sized legal or medical firm

Skills and Abilities:
- Excellent communicator
- Intelligent
- Able to handle stressful situations
- Patient with people in all situations
- Fluent in English and Spanish
- Respectful of privacy
- Self-disciplined
- Able to summarize information correctly

Here is a third list of Anna's skills and abilities. This list highlights the skills a cashier would need. Notice that she has added some new skills to the list. The new skills are more important to the job of cashier than to the job of telecommunicator.

Objective: Cashier position with a retail business

Skills and Abilities:
- Excellent mathematics skills
- Pleasant and polite
- Quick learner
- Able to handle stressful situations and situations that require quick action
- Self-starter
- Excellent communicator
- Intelligent
- Fluent in English and Spanish

When you create more than one version of your résumé, give each version a separate but memorable filename. (Anna named her files *resume-telecom, resume-receptionist* and *resume-cashier.*) Print just the version you need.

Look back at the résumé you created on page 42. What other job could you apply for? In the form below, change your résumé to fit another opportunity. Write a new objective, and then revise the rest of the résumé to fit that job.

_____

_____

_____

_____

_____

Objective: _____

Experience: _____

_____

_____

_____

_____

Education: _____

_____

_____

Skills: _____   _____

_____   _____

_____   _____

_____   _____

Volunteer Work and Honors/Awards: _____

_____

_____

References available upon request.

Finding a Job: The Cover Letter

What: A letter that will attract the attention of a possible employer

Audience: Anyone who might consider hiring you

Purpose: To be invited for an interview and then hired

Sometimes you can get a job interview by phoning an employer or by going to the company in person. While you are there, you might be asked to fill out a special application form.

However, many employers will ask for a written application before they will consider you for an interview. Also, you may need to send a written application if you want a job in a new location. A written application includes both a cover letter and a résumé.

Your letter is the first thing an employer will see, so write it carefully. It introduces you and tells why you are applying for the job. It gives you an opportunity to highlight aspects of your experience or education that are especially important for a particular job. Since the letter will be sent with your résumé, it doesn't need to cover everything.

Here are some pointers for job application letters:

- Follow business-letter form (see page 18).

- In the first sentence, name the job you are applying for. If you saw an ad for the job somewhere, tell where you saw it.

- Next, tell why you are qualified for the job. Mention any related work experience that you have. Specify the skills you have that make you an excellent candidate for this job.

- You may want to include the names, addresses, phone numbers, and e-mail addresses of one or two references in your letter. A reference is a person who knows you well but is not part of your family. Listing a current or former boss or teacher is a good idea. Choose people who can speak positively about you.

- Before you give a potential reference's name to a possible employer, ask whether he or she is willing to act as a reference for you.

- Proofread very carefully. Find and fix all spelling, punctuation, and grammar errors.

- Always respond to want ads as quickly as possible. You want your application to be one of the first to arrive.

- Put your letter on top of your résumé when you fill the envelope.

Here is a job application letter.

117 West Second Street
St. Thomas, CO 80513
August 29, 2006

Manager
Candlewood Gardens Apartments
1300 Candlewood Drive
Bickville, CO 80522

Dear Manager:

With this letter, I would like to apply for the assistant manager position you advertised in the August 27 *Daily Coloradan*.

For the past four years, I have managed the maintenance and rental office of Second Street Apartments in St. Thomas. I have handled all routine maintenance for the property, a seven-story building with 42 apartments. In addition, I have supervised reroofing and replacement of the building's heating system. Rentals have been consistent. Under my management, no apartment has stood empty for more than one month.

Now I would like to bring my skills to a broader management position in a larger apartment complex. The enclosed resume summarizes my experience in more detail. I would welcome the opportunity to talk with you and look forward to hearing from you soon.

Sincerely,

Rafael Brown

Rafael Brown

1. Write a job application cover letter

Look back at the personal data sheet and résumé you wrote in Lesson 6. Then look at a recent newspaper employment section. Pick out an ad for a job you would like to have and for which you might be qualified. Write an application letter for that job in the form below.

2. Responding to want ads

Read the want ads below. For each ad, decide what you should do *first*. Underline the part of the ad that tells you. Then mark the right answer.

A.

ASSISTANT WANTED. Need bright person to assist me in my fast-growing businesses. 4 hours/day, 5 days/week. Call 489-3251 for appointment, 8-11 a.m.

_____ **a.** Telephone

_____ **b.** Send application letter and résumé

_____ **c.** Apply in person

B.

SALESPERSON. no exp. nec. Must have own car. Salary plus commission. Send application letter to Box C-34, Daily News.

_____ **a.** Telephone

_____ **b.** Send application letter and résumé

_____ **c.** Apply in person

C.

CLERK. Filing, phone, familiarity with Office 2000. Apply at personnel office, 4th floor, Brown Insurance Co., 721 W. 54th Ave., 9-5.

_____ **a.** Telephone

_____ **b.** Send application letter and résumé

_____ **c.** Apply in person

D.

FRY COOK. Nights, 8 p.m.-1 a.m. Apply at Burger Heaven, 1451 E. Water St., 2-4 p.m.

_____ **a.** Telephone

_____ **b.** Send application letter and résumé

_____ **c.** Apply in person

E.

ASSEMBLERS. Light production work. Full time. No exp. req. Interviews by appt. only. Contact Mr. Wilson, 770-6141.

_____ **a.** Telephone

_____ **b.** Send application letter and résumé

_____ **c.** Apply in person

F.

RECREATION AIDE. Supervise and schedule team sports, work with volunteers. Sports exp. req. Must relate well to children. Send resume to Gerald Holmes, Westvale Boys Club, 3445 Westvale Ave., Oakdale, VT 11245.

_____ **a.** Telephone

_____ **b.** Send application letter and résumé

_____ **c.** Apply in person

Using the Internet in a Job Search

What: Job-search help sites, online newspaper want ads, and job list sites

Audience: Employers who are hiring

Purpose: To be invited for an interview or hired for a job

The Internet can be helpful when you are looking for a job. Use it to find advice on many aspects of the job search:

- writing résumés
- writing job application letters
- interviewing for jobs

You can also use the Internet to find announcements of job opportunities.

- Many web sites list job opportunities. To find these, use a web tool like Google. Search for the words *job search*. You will see a long list of sites showing open jobs.

- Many newspapers publish their want ad pages online. Want ads are especially helpful if you know what kind of work you want. If you will be moving, look online at newspapers in the new area.

- If you would like to work for a particular business, look for its web site. Then look for a link labeled *Employment,* or *We're Hiring,* or *Job Opportunities.* Click the link to learn how to apply for a job with that business. You might be asked to send a letter, or you might be invited to call or visit the business.

Why use the Internet in your search? You can use it any time, day or night. You can look for jobs nearby or far away. When you tell a potential employer that you found the job listing on the Internet, that employer knows that you can use a computer.

Before You Begin

Before you begin looking on the Internet, think about what you want to find. Here are things to consider:

- What job do you want?
- What skills do you have?
- Who do you want to work for?
- Where do you want to work?

Here is Hakim's list of answers to these questions. He can use the underlined words and phrases to search online. Typing *Oakland CA* focuses his search on jobs available in Oakland, CA.

Here are some results from Hakim's search. He entered *construction jobs Oakland CA* in the search box.

After you have done a search, look at the web sites. If you find a job that interests you on a site, look for application instructions.

Check the Job List Web Site

You want to be sure you have found a safe web site. Look for these things.

- Does the web site show a date, and has it been updated recently?
- Is the web site reliable? Does it tell about the people who run it? Does it include contact information for those people?
- Does the web site charge a fee? Many are free. Is this site worth paying for?
- Do site owners respond to a request for more information? If they don't, be very cautious.

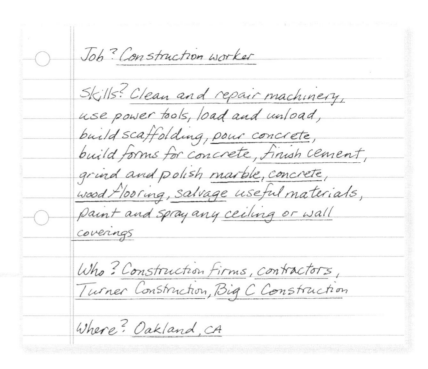

Be Secure

Protect your personal information, just as you would if you were ordering products online. Some job search sites allow you to type information about yourself. Others charge a fee for their services. When you need to enter personal information in situations like these, enter as little as you can. The site will tell you what is required. Also, make sure the site is secure. The address for a secure web site begins *https://* instead of the usual *http://*.

LESSON 8: Activity

Complete the form below. Use the data sheet you created on page 41. Then underline any words or phrases that you could use in an Internet search.

What job do you want? _____

What skills do you have? _____

_____

_____

_____

_____

Who do you want to work for? _____

_____

_____

_____

Where do you want to work? _____

Reaching the Public

What: News or information that will be seen by the public

Audience: The public—people you know and people you don't know

Purpose: To sell something, tell about something lost or found,
or share information about an event

Here are some reasons why you might want to let many people know about something:

- You want to buy or sell an item.
- You have lost or found something valuable.
- You are offering a service for hire.
- You want to invite the public to an event.

How do you make this kind of information available to the general public? There are several ways to go about it.

Newspaper Want Ads

Newspaper wants ads are a good way to advertise. A small ad can cost very little, and many people may see it.

Choosing the paper

A city may have one or two large daily papers. It may also have some small weekly papers that serve individual neighborhoods. In small towns, there is likely to be only one paper. Some news companies also publish weekly advertising supplements featuring private want ads and business advertising.

Here are guidelines for deciding where to place your ad:

- If you are selling something small, choose a local paper or an advertising supplement. People are not likely to travel far to buy something used and small.

- If you are selling a large, expensive item—like your car— then think big. People might travel farther to purchase a car. Place an ad in the large city newspaper or in the papers of neighboring towns.

Placing the ad

You can call a newspaper to place an ad. If you know the name of the newspaper, get the number from the white pages of the phone book. If not, look in the yellow pages under *Newspapers*. When you call, ask for the classified ad department. Find out:

- how much the ad will cost. You may be charged by the word or by the line.

- the deadline for placing the ad. Newspapers have strict deadlines. Submit your ad well before the deadline.

Writing your ad

There are two main things to remember when you write a want ad:

- Keep it short to keep the cost down.
- Make it clear so that readers know exactly what you are describing.

Put the most important thing first. Are you selling something? Name it first. Do you have a service to offer? Say that first. Then add any explanation that is needed.

Here are some want ads from a local paper. Notice that they are organized by subject. Notice also that many of the words are abbreviated. If you pay by the line, an ad with abbreviated words will cost you less.

Include your phone number if you want people to call you about your ad. Include your address if you want them to come to your home—for a garage sale, for example.

If you do not want people to contact you directly, the newspaper can help. Many newspapers have mail boxes set aside for the use of advertising customers. The newspaper will give you a box number to use in your ad. You will be charged for this service.

12 LOST

IRISH SETTER PUP 5 mos. Answers to Kelly. Lost in W. Elmwood area. Please call 489-9811. Reward.

SUNGLASSES prescription lady's, black frames. Elmwood library eve of Aug 15. Call 456-3400.

18 AUTOS FOR SALE

1997 BUICK LESABRE. Custom, 106,000 miles. $3495 obo. Call 213-446-7199.

2004 PONTIAC BONNEVILLE, SSE1, loaded. $14800. Call 213-478-2336.

1999 CHEVY S10 BLAZER, LS, dk green, 4WD, 86k, PL, PW, AC, PS, cruise, tilt. Very clean. 213-446-1778.

69 HOME FURNISHINGS

PINE TABLE Finished, 38 x 48. Like new, $50. 213-478-6625.

69 HOME FURNISHINGS

WHIRPOOL WASHER AND DRYER Heavy duty super capacity. 7 years old. Excellent condition. $350 obo. Call 213-776-1589.

71 GARAGE SALES

BIG MULTI FAMILY SALE. 450-453 Grace Place, Jamesville. Sat. & Sun. 8-5. Toys, clothes, household goods, exercise equip, tools, & lots more.

MOVING SALE All must go. 3055 Delaware, Centertown. May 2 and 3, 8-3.

93 SERVICES

LAWN CARE Will mow residential, commercial, or lake lots. High-weed mowing available. Reasonble rates and free estimates. 213-478-9076.

TILE INSTALLATION Floors, walls, showers professionally installed. Locally owned. 213-776-8843.

Posters

Another way to reach the public is by making a poster. A poster can be used to advertise many things:

- items for sale, such as cars or houses
- garage sales or other sales of used items (rummage sales, tag sales, lawn sales, etc.)
- events for your organization, such as fund-raisers, concerts, or programs
- a service you are offering, such as baby-sitting or lawn care

What should the poster say?

- Be sure to tell *who, what, where,* and *when.*
- If you are selling something, you may want to include *the price.*
- If you're inviting people to an event, say *who* is sponsoring the event, who is performing, and maybe even who can come.
- If the event costs money, include the ticket price.

Here are two posters. Do they include everything you need to know?

Making a poster

You can make one poster by drawing with colored pens and markers on heavy paper. If you want many copies, draw the poster on a sheet of paper, or design it on a computer. Then make copies of it on a copy machine.

Artwork, interesting lettering, and bright colors can make your poster stand out.

Where to put posters

Choose places where many people will see them. Libraries, malls, or neighborhood stores are usually good locations. Be sure to ask for permission to hang your poster.

The Elmwood Family Council Presents a Community Dance!

Fun for the Whole Family!

♪♪♪ Live Music by ♪♪♪
The Wholesome String Band

Juniper Elementary School Gymnasium

414 Elm St.

October 10   7:30-10:00 p.m.

$5 general admission; $3 students and seniors

Baby-sitting Service
My home or yours
12 years' experience
Certified with County Extension
Loving, fun, respectful!
Call now! 218-476-9924

Baby sitting 218-476-9924
Baby sitting 218-476-9924
Baby sitting 218-476-9924
Baby sitting 218-476-9924
Baby sitting 218-476-9924
Baby sitting 218-476-9924
Baby sitting 218-476-9924
Baby sitting 218-476-9924

Press Releases

Clubs, organizations, and church groups often invite the public to events they are sponsoring. How do they let the public know about their events? Of course, they can make and display posters. But to reach a wider audience, they can send press releases.

A press release informs newspaper editors about an event. An editor may publish a press release as written but often will edit it.

Here is the press release that was written to go with the first poster on page 56.

Writing a press release isn't as hard as it sounds. These are the basic rules.

1. First, write an attention-grabbing headline and list the specific details.

   - WHO: Give the exact name of your group.

   - WHAT: Give a basic description of the event.

   - WHERE: Give the street address. You may need to add more information, such as a room number or directions.

   - WHEN: Give the date and time. Include the ending time if there is a definite end.

2. Next, write a short publicity article about the event. Include all the details that you put at the top, but add more information.

   - Say more about the event or the performers.

   - For a fund-raiser, explain the reason.

   - If tickets are needed, tell where they can be purchased and what they cost.

   - Give a contact name and number to call for more information about the event.

3. Last, include your name, phone number, and e-mail address (if you have one). The editor will contact you if there are questions.

4. End the release with three number signs.

FOR IMMEDIATE RELEASE

Elmwood Family Council presents dance and night out

WHO: The Elmwood Family Council
WHAT: Community Dance with The Wholesome String Band
WHERE: Juniper Elementary School Gymnasium, 414 Elm St.
WHEN: October 10, 7:30-10:00 p.m.

The Elmwood Family Council will present a community dance next Friday, October 10, from 7:30 to 10:00 p.m. at Juniper Elementary School.

Tickets for the event cost $5 for general admission and $3 for students and seniors. The dance will be held in the Juniper Elementary School Gymnasium at 414 Elm Street in Elmwood. Music and dancing start at 7:30 p.m. and will last until 10:00 p.m.

The community dance will feature the Wholesome String Band. They have been playing together for ten years and specialize in the music of Ireland and Appalachia. Members of the band include Ian McEachron on fiddle, Julia Simms on bass, Geordie Mack on accordian, and Gordon James on flutes and bagpipes. Sarah Whortle will call the dances.

The Elmwood Family Council is a nonprofit organization working to strengthen families in the Elmwood community. It holds events for families and provides free counseling to parents and children at its offices on Main Street. For more information about the community dance or the Elmwood Family Council, call LaDonna James at 443-2178.

CONTACT: LaDonna James, Director
         Elmwood Family Council
         443-2178
         or e-mail efc@familiesmatter.org

#   #   #

1. Write a want ad

Write a want ad to sell an item. Make up all the details you need. For ideas, look at page 55.

_____

_____

_____

2. Write a press release

Write a press release for one of these events. Make up all the details.

- Your organization is holding a concert.
- Your organization is announcing its annual meeting.
- Your club is holding a car wash to raise money.

FOR IMMEDIATE RELEASE

HEADLINE: _____

WHO: _____

WHAT: _____

WHERE: _____

WHEN: _____

_____

_____

_____

_____

_____

CONTACT: _____

_____

\#   \#   \#

Using the Computer in Daily Life

What: E-mail, instant messages, and blogs

Audience: Friends, family, and people who share your interests

Purpose: To share news, ideas, and opinions

For many people, the Internet has become an important way to keep in touch.

You can use e-mail to write short or long notes to friends and family. E-mail discussion lists are a way to "talk" online to people who have interests similar to yours. Instant messaging allows you to "talk" in real time to someone else. And blogs, or web logs, allow you to share your thoughts with the public.

All you need to get started is a computer. Many public libraries have computers available for anyone to use. Usually you must sign up to use one.

Remember that the Internet is public. When you send e-mail to a discussion list or publish a blog you can't control who will read or forward what you have written. Your writing will also be stored electronically, often for a long time. Use your best judgment about what to write.

Communicating Over the Internet

Using e-mail

To send e-mail, you need to connect to the Internet. You can usually do that at a public library, where it is free. However, if you use the Internet at home, you must pay for an Internet connection.

E-mail is set up separately from an Internet connection. Free e-mail services, such as Hotmail, are available to anyone. Your librarian can help you start. Once you have an e-mail address, you can write to anyone else with an e-mail address.

Here is an example of an e-mail message.

Notice what it includes:

- The e-mail address of the person you are writing to. You must type this in.
- The subject of the e-mail. This lets the other person know what the message is about.
- Your message.

When you e-mail friends and family, write as if you were writing a personal note.

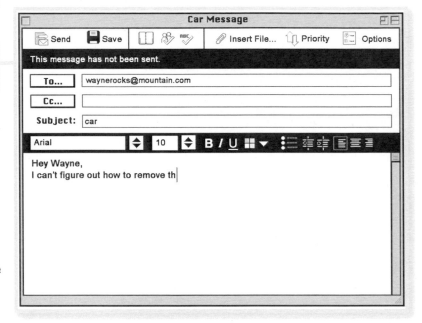

Joining an e-mail discussion list

E-mail lists connect people who share an interest. A list is created around a topic. List topics cover everything from art to zoology. Anyone who shares interest in a list's topic can join. When you join a list, you receive all the e-mails sent by members of the list. When you send an e-mail to the list, all other list members receive it.

In this way, you become part of an ongoing discussion about a topic. Lists are also used to pass on information, such as recipes, news about medications, or vacation tips.

How can you join a discussion list? First, find a list that interests you. Use a search engine like Google, and search for *email lists.* You will find sites that list many e-mail discussion lists. Choose a list you like.

To join, send an e-mail to the host of the list. You will be asked to type a direction, for instance *subscribe rangersfans-L,* into either the subject field or the body of the e-mail. You may also be asked to include your name. Follow the instructions exactly. When you send the e-mail, you will be added to the discussion list automatically.

Sending instant messages

Instant messaging is like talking on the telephone, except that you write instead of talking. When you use an instant-messaging program, you send typed messages directly to another person. The other person types a message right back. There is no delay.

The other person must use the same instant-messaging program you do. Several are available. AOL and MSN are two of the most popular instant-messaging hosts.

Here are instant messages sent by two friends, Luis and Wayne. They write to each other as if they were talking. Notice that they don't worry about punctuation or spelling. It's all very casual.

Signing up for instant messaging is easy. Just go to a host site, such as Yahoo, AOL, or MSN. Find the link labeled *Messenger* and select it. Follow instructions. Soon you will be sending instant messages to your friends.

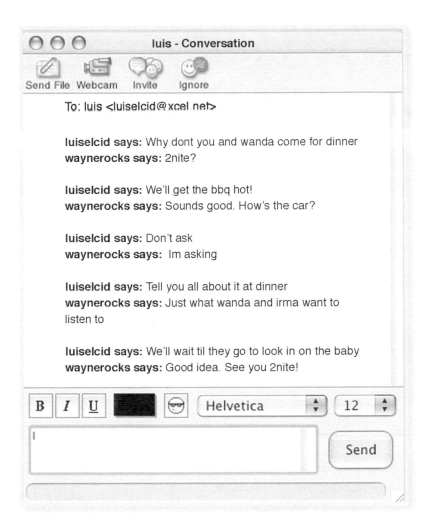

To: luis <luiselcid@xcel net>

luiselcid says: Why dont you and wanda come for dinner
waynerocks says: 2nite?

luiselcid says: We'll get the bbq hot!
waynerocks says: Sounds good. How's the car?

luiselcid says: Don't ask
waynerocks says: Im asking

luiselcid says: Tell you all about it at dinner
waynerocks says: Just what wanda and irma want to listen to

luiselcid says: We'll wait til they go to look in on the baby
waynerocks says: Good idea. See you 2nite!

Using abbreviations

In e-mail and instant messages, people often use abbreviations. This makes writing faster. It can also be fun. But if you don't know what the abbreviations stand for, it can be frustrating.

Here are some of the most commonly used abbreviations.

Typed words in an e-mail can't show how you feel about what you are saying. So people have come up with special character combinations, called emoticons, to display feelings.

Here are a few common emoticons.

To emphasize a word, write it all in capital letters. However, avoid writing every word in capital letters. This is considered to be shouting and is generally disliked.

Here is an e-mail that uses many abbreviations. See if you can read it.

E-mail Abbreviations

B4	before
BRB	be right back
BTW	by the way
CUL8R	see you later
FYI	for your information
GA	go ahead
GMTA	great minds think alike
ILY	I love you
IMHO	in my humble opinion
LOL	laughing out loud
OTOH	on the other hand
ROTFL	rolling on the floor laughing

Emoticons

:-)	smile	:- (	frown
;-)	smile with a wink	<g>	grin

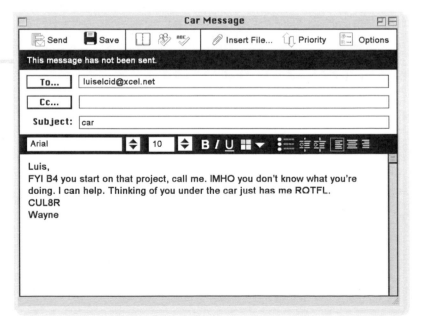

Car Message

Send   Save   Insert File...   Priority   Options

This message has not been sent.

To... luiselcid@xcel.net

Cc...

Subject: car

Arial   10   B I U

Luis,
FYI B4 you start on that project, call me. IMHO you don't know what you're doing. I can help. Thinking of you under the car just has me ROTFL.
CUL8R
Wayne

Blogs

A blog, or web log, is an online journal or diary. Blogs were first created in 1999. Now, there are millions of them. Anyone can have a blog.

People start blogs for many reasons:

- to keep a public diary
- to share news and photographs (for instance, about a wedding or a new baby)
- to share opinions about a topic

There are blogs about everything—politics, sports, pets, you name it.

How to start your own blog

Why do you want your own blog? Choose a topic that interests you and that you will still be interested in months from now.

Then find a web site that will help you set up your blog. Type *start a blog* into the search box on a search engine like Google.

Starting a blog is easy, like setting up an e-mail address or joining an instant-messaging service. Choose a name for your blog, and you're ready to go.

A successful blog is unique and interesting. Change the content on your blog as often as possible—even every day. Remember, though, that anyone can read a blog. Be careful what you write about!

Here is a blog by Shelly, a new mother. Shelly's family lives far away, and her blog is a way for her to stay connected with them.

If you want a fancier blog than the service provides, you'll need to learn more about computer programming. But for beginners, a free blog service is an easy, enjoyable, and inexpensive way to get started.

Kayla Is Here!

Yesterday the doctor gave Kayla a clean bill of health. She just gets more and more beautiful.

Here she is sleeping. I sang the same lullaby my own father sang to me. Kayla fell right to sleep. Then I got busy! While Kayla sleeps I try to get as much done as I can. There is no rest for the weary!

Here is Kayla when she saw another baby for the first time. My friend Tomoko came with her son. Kayla seemed happy to have a friend! I never imagined how important other people would be in a baby's life.

1. Write an e-mail

Write an e-mail message to a friend. Use some abbreviations (see page 62).

Message
To...
Cc...
Subject:

2. Plan a blog

Use the form below to begin planning your own blog. Think about what you have to say that would be of interest to other people.

Possible topic: _____

What I know about the topic: _____

_____

_____

_____

Three things about the topic that I would like to learn more about: _____

_____

_____

Possible title for my blog: _____